Loyd Corder:
Traveler for God

EUGENE CHAMBERLAIN
Illustrated by Ron Hester

1036

BROADMAN PRESS
Nashville, Tennessee

To the "Texas River Rats," especially to those who are my personal friends: Marigene, Carol, Cyndi, Brian, Neal, Susan, and Vicki

The "Texas River Rats" are college students who serve Jesus Christ in the Rio Grande valley each summer. They preach, sing, teach the Bible, and help people learn to read and write. In fact, they do anything they can to help Mexicans on both sides of the river. They work with the Texas Baptist Rio Grande River Ministry. "River Rats" is a nickname they gave themselves.

This book is dedicated to them for two reasons. First, they helped me better understand the importance of mission work with Spanish-speaking people. Second, the work done by such young people helps fulfill a dream of Dr. Loyd Corder—and this book is all about Dr. Corder and how he helped and still helps Spanish-speaking people know Jesus Christ as their Savior.

© Copyright 1983 • Broadman Press
All rights reserved.
4242-84
ISBN: 0-8054-4284-7
Dewey Decimal Classification: J266.092
Subject Headings: CORDER, LOYD // MISSIONS, HOME
Library of Congress Catalog Card Number: 82-73663
Printed in the United States of America

Contents

The Beginning 5

Plainview PK 10

The Garrison Year 20

Abilene and Robert Lee 24

The Stockdale Years 30

College, Romance, and Marriage 34

A New Life Together 42

The San Antonio Years 46

The Atlanta Years 51

Beyond Retirement 61

Remember 64

About the Author 64

The Beginning

On March 4, 1916, a chill New Mexico wind swept down from the north. There was nothing between the plains and the North Pole except a barbed-wire fence, and it was down. James Alexander Corder stood on the south side of the two-room, boxed house to get some warmth from the mild March sun. Still he shivered. But he could not bring himself to go inside.

Not now. Inside the house his young wife was giving birth to their first child.

To forget his worry, he recalled the long wagon trip that had brought him and his parents to New Mexico. They were a farm family who came west to homestead in the territory of New Mexico. That was in 1912, the same year that New Mexico became a state.

Jim's thoughts ended abruptly. A baby's cry came over the sound of the wind. Jim leaped toward the door just as his mother opened it. "You have a boy, a fine boy," she announced.

Benjamin Loyd Corder had drawn his first breath. And he was ready for life. No one had the faintest idea where life would take him. They could not know the roads he would follow across the plains of Texas and along its streams and rivers. No one thought of his living in towns that would one day be great cities of the Southwest. Certainly his parents did not dream that Loyd would be known throughout much of the country. Nor did they think he would travel the entire United States and countries beyond the farthest horizons. No one could foresee that the tiny fists, clenching and unclenching, would someday control the flight of a plane across the blue sky above the wide, wide prairie.

But both James Alexander and Clara Elnora Sharry Corder

believed that God had something special in store for their infant son. Jim lifted the baby from Clara's arms. He grinned at the baby. Reaching one hand toward his wife's outstretched hand, he bowed his head. The prayer he prayed was for both of them.

"We thank you, Lord, for this fine son. We dedicate him to your service, Lord. Guide his steps and use him according to your will. In Jesus' name. Amen."

Loyd Corder was truly a son of the fast-vanishing American frontier. His father and mother met four years before his birth. Benjamin Carvin Sharry had brought his family to the territory of New Mexico the same year the Corders had arrived.

The Corders and the Sharrys soon built permanent houses. These houses were called boxed houses. The walls were constructed of a single thickness of boards. Each board, twelve inches wide and one inch thick, stood in a vertical position. Its bottom was nailed to the framing on which the floor of the house rested. Its top was nailed to the framing that supported the roof. Cracks always existed between the boards. To make the houses more nearly wind and weatherproof, long narrow boards were nailed along each crack.

There was no inner wall. Paper was pasted over the inside of the planks for further protection against the weather. The cold winds of winter chilled one's bones. The hot winds of the long summers burned the skin and eyes. A family needed all the protection it could manage.

Loyd Corder was born in just such a boxed house. The house was one of about a half-dozen such houses scattered over the community. There was no real town.

Later the village of Lingo sprang up as a center for the hardy homesteaders. There were a post office, a school, a blacksmith shop, and one or two churches in Lingo. When the automobile came into its own, there was even a filling station.

You will not find Lingo on a current map. The original settlers died out, moved to other places, or retreated to the settled lands from which they came.

Tending a cotton crop on the newly-broken prairie was, in many

ways, as much woman's work as man's. Clara Corder took her place in the field alongside her husband. And Loyd's coming into the family could not be allowed to interrupt their teamwork.

"I'm intending to be back in the field with you tomorrow, Jim," Clara said at the supper table one late, spring evening.

Exhausted from his day of hard work, Jim could scarcely believe his ears. "But how do you plan to take care of young Loyd?" he exclaimed.

Clara replied with a grin. "You'll see."

Soon after breakfast the next morning, Jim went to the field. Clara cleared away the breakfast dishes and readied the lunch she would share with Jim in the field at noon.

Then wrapping Loyd in a soft quilt, she stepped through the open doorway into the full sunlight. Whistling to Trixie, the family dog, she set out to join her husband. At the edge of the field, she dropped to her knees. Carefully cradling Loyd against her slim shoulder, she shook open the quilt. Then she laid Loyd on it, smoothing the quilt to its full size.

Getting back to her feet, Clara smiled down at the baby. Then she looked at Trixie. "Stay with Loyd," she commanded the small dog.

As she moved away, she heard a faint yap. She looked back to see Trixie settling down beside the happy, gurgling baby. Clara knew she could depend on Trixie to protect Loyd from ants, beetles, and even snakes.

The Corders' days seemed much alike. They worked hard to bring in good cotton crops, to grow a garden, and to tend their orchard. The birth of a girl, Carrie, was the next big event of their lives. The year was 1918.

Then when Loyd was only three years old, everything changed. Jim Corder awoke one morning with a fever. He knew this was no ordinary fever.

"It's typhoid," Grandmother Corder breathed when she was summoned to the house.

"Typhoid!" Clara whispered with fear. "What are we to do?" she asked her white-faced mother-in-law. "What are we to do?"

8

"Well, Dear," Grandmother Corder responded, "the first thing is to get all of you over to our house."

Young Loyd was more bewildered than frightened. His grandparents' home was a familiar place, and he felt at home there. At his age he could not count off the fifty-two days his father lay in bed. The first days were shadowed by the fear which gripped his mother and grandparents. But in time the bad experience was only a memory for them, as well as for Loyd.

The fifty-two days marked a turning point in Jim Corder's life. And that meant a turning point in Loyd's life too. During his illness, Jim had many hours to think and to pray. He spent a lot of time doing both. He realized that God was calling him to become a preacher. Loyd was just about to become a PK, a "preacher's kid."

Plainview PK

Jim Corder's long illness and even longer time of recovery were difficult days. But following through on his surrender to the ministry was more difficult. He was a twenty-two-year-old man with a wife, a four-year-old son, a baby daughter, and a farm. He had plenty of responsibilities. What he did not have was a proper education.

Jim knew that he had to get an education. But how? And where? He needed a place where he could complete high school and work toward a college degree.

Some Texas Baptists in the panhandle town of Plainview had opened Wayland Academy and Junior College. Soon Jim Corder had arranged to enter eighth grade. He planned to stay in Plainview through two years of college.

Within a few weeks of Jim's acceptance at Wayland Academy, the Corders were living in Plainview. Their new home was a small house on the short street called Preachers' Row. Nearly every house on the street sheltered a family like their own. It wasn't a bad place to live, except not one house had running water. And the nearest source of water was some distance away!

The residents of Preachers' Row solved the problem. Someone suggested digging a well of their own—right in the middle of the block. At first it was only a wild idea. But soon they were all saying, "Why not? We really could do it."

Every student preacher who lived on the Row, as well as some others, joined in the dig. Their "drill" consisted of a heavy bit made of pipe. The pipe was attached by a rope to the short end of a long pump handle. The handle itself rode on a steel pin between

10

two sturdy wooden posts. When the drilling crew pushed down on the long end of the handle, the pipe would rise a few inches.

When the crew leader yelled, "Let 'er go," everyone released the handle at the same time. The pipe fell to the bottom of the hole. With each drop, the pipe was driven a few inches deeper into the hole.

After several hours of drilling, every crew member was sweaty and tired. "Can you imagine moving along after digging a well as Isaac did?" one of the men exclaimed.

"No sirree," breathed another, wiping the back of his hand across his eyes to clear away the sweat.

But after a time the drill broke through to water. Then the men forgot their aching muscles and dirty hands. Caps flew into the air along with a chorus of hurrahs.

Washday from then on was an exciting time. Each family assembled to pump the water needed for its household. Mother, father, and every child big enough to carry even a small bucket joined in carrying the water to their house.

One day Jim rushed into the Corder house on Preachers' Row. "Guess what!" he exclaimed. "I've got a regular job."

Wayland Academy kept a dairy herd to provide milk for its dining hall. Jim was to be in charge of the cows. The Corders already had a cow of their own, so the school let them pasture her with the herd. Whatever else the Corders lacked, they always had plenty of milk.

Another part of the job was to feed the school's hogs with food left over from the dining room. When fall came, the biting wind swept down across the high plains. It brought crisp and clear days with freezing temperatures. Hog-killing time had come. Loyd offered to help his dad.

"Well, Son," Pop replied somewhat doubtfully, "hog-killing isn't the prettiest business in the world. And it's hard work."

"I can do it. I can. See how big I am." Loyd's blue eyes were bright with enthusiasm. He flexed his right arm to show his muscle. But Pop only smiled and allowed Loyd to go with him.

As the afternoon wore on, Loyd's confidence in his hog-killing skills wavered. When the men slit the hog open and began to remove all of the insides, Loyd lit out for home.

Some fathers might have teased a boy in such circumstances. Pop chose not to. When he reached home, he showed Loyd the fresh meat he had brought. "Hog-killing isn't easy, Son," he said. "But it's worth the effort. That's the way with most things that amount to much."

Loyd was inclined to agree. Fresh pork was a welcome break from the pinto beans and corn bread which made up the greater part of the family diet.

During the summer months Pop always managed to hold several revival meetings. He took the family along with him to these meetings. Revival days were good days because the farm families lived well. Every family who entertained the preacher and his family served the biggest and richest meals their pantries and gardens could yield.

Loyd and Carrie had fun playing with the children in the homes they visited. One family even had a pet donkey. Moving that donkey out and away from the barn was not easy.

"Beat him, Loyd. Beat him," the son of the house yelled.

Loyd thought he was already beating the animal half to death. But he raised his arm once more, gritted his teeth, and gave the donkey the mightiest whack he could.

The donkey went ambling away from the barn. He acted as if he had wanted to take Loyd for a ride all along.

"Now, turn him," the friend's voice rang out.

Glancing over his shoulder, Loyd was surprised to see how far he and his mount had come. He swung the donkey's head back toward the barn.

Suddenly that plodding creature became a madly charging steed. He dashed for the barn with Loyd hanging to his neck. With his brown hair streaming across his eyes, Loyd was barely able to keep his seat. He wondered if riding a donkey for fun were worth the effort. When Loyd arrived safely at the barn, he decided it was. It was a whole lot more pleasant than hog-killing.

In April of 1923 another baby girl was added to the Corder

13

family. Loyd's second sister was named Leota Blanche. The family called her Dikki.

When Loyd was seven, he enrolled at Central Grade School. His parents proudly took him to the two-story, red-brick building on the first day.

The second day he put on his best blue-denim overalls and a clean, white, cotton shirt. Loyd's mother checked his sturdy black shoes to be sure they were clean, even though they were scuffed. Then Loyd bravely set off for Central School and Miss Stubblefield's first-grade room. After that he walked more than a mile each way every school day in Plainview.

After four years on Preachers' Row, the Corders moved to a larger house a mile or so farther west. The year was 1925, and Loyd was just nine. Already the spring winds were promising the great dust storms of the 1930's. The winds picked up sand from plowed fields. For three days and nights the winds dashed grit against walls, windows, and doors. The front gate disappeared behind the dirty curtain.

At night sleep seemed impossible. But Clara Corder, resourceful as ever, came up with an idea. If netting could protect sleepers from mosquitoes, then a sheet could protect them from the sand. She draped sheets over the four bed posts. And the family was able to get some sleep.

But the air was not warmed by the dust which filled it. Coal had to be brought in if meals were to be cooked and if the family were to stay warm.

"Loyd, I want you to go out to the coal pile and bring a bucket of coal in here," Pop said toward the end of the first day of the storm.

Loyd wrapped a scarf over his face and pulled his cap low before starting out the door. He was dismayed when he reached the coal pile. It was already more than half-buried under a miniature sand dune. By the time Loyd collected enough coal for the evening's fire, he also had a lot of useless sand.

"Pop, how are we going to use this sandy coal?" Loyd asked.

Pop scratched his head a minute. Then he had an idea. He fastened some screen to a frame he made. Loyd jiggled the coal back and forth on the screen, sifting the sand away. For the next three or four days Loyd sifted every bucket of coal they used.

After the third day, the winds fell until all was quiet once more. Then Clara Corder examined her house. Dust was everywhere. On tables. On floors. On chairs. Under tables. Under chairs. In closets. And it was more than an inch deep!

Pop and Loyd weren't the only Corders who went to school in Plainview. Mrs. Corder studied Spanish. One day she and Loyd went shopping. As they walked down the street, they passed a group of Mexican farm workers. The workers were talking with one another in their own language.

"Why are they talking so funny, Mommie?" Loyd whispered. "Are they all right?"

"Loyd, they are speaking in Spanish. That is their native language. They came from Mexico where everyone talks Spanish. English is our native language," she explained.

For the first time Loyd realized that there are people of many races and who speak different languages.

At times Loyd thought, "I don't always do what is right even when I know I should. My actions don't show what I truly believe about right and wrong."

"I know to obey Pop and Mommie," Loyd muttered to himself. "But I don't always do it. And sometimes I don't exactly tell the truth. I get to telling something that happened at school. Before I know it, I'm making the whole story more exciting than it really was." Loyd's clear blue eyes seemed to darken as he continued this talk with himself.

"And I'm not supposed to fight with my sister. But Carrie makes me mad sometimes. And then we do have a real brawl."

"And don't forget that fight you had with Clifton Tennison," his conscience told him. "And you are always taking cookies and other goodies out of Mommie's kitchen when she isn't looking."

The more Loyd considered these ideas, the more bothered he became. One day he talked to his mother about these feelings. He wanted her to show him how to handle them.

"Loyd," his mother began, "you know that the Bible teaches we

16

must obey God. Now you are finding out that it is impossible for a person to be what he should be without God's help." She knew Loyd was under conviction about his sins. She knew he was troubled when he misbehaved.

Together they talked about why Jesus came into the world. They discussed what a person must do to become a follower of Jesus. Patiently Mommie helped Loyd understand God's plan for forgiving people of their sins and for giving them new lives through their faith in Jesus Christ.

Loyd easily understood what his mother was saying. At least he understood it with his mind. But he was still not ready to accept Christ as his Lord and Savior.

One summer Pop Corder preached a revival in the country church where he was pastor. Of course, the entire Corder family attended every service. Loyd had a hard time staying awake during the evening services. Sometimes only the cool prairie wind kept Loyd awake when the kerosene lamps flickered.

But in one daytime service, Loyd listened quietly to every word his father spoke. As he listened, something wonderful happened to him. He understood the plan of salvation with his whole being, not just with his head. The invitation was given at the end of the service. Loyd stepped out into the narrow aisle. He walked toward his smiling father. That day Loyd made his profession of faith.

When his father presented him to the church, Loyd brushed back the fine brown hair that was forever slipping down his forehead. He smiled and his eyes were bright with joy. After the service, the church people shook his hand and told him how happy they were about his decision to become a follower of Jesus. But Mommie hugged him close to her, and he squeezed her hard.

That day seemed different from any other day in Loyd's life. On the way home Loyd tried to explain how he felt. "This doesn't even seem like the same day," he said. "The sun was shining when we went to church. But now it seems like the sun is brighter. And there are more butterflies. More sunshine. More flowers. Everything is so beautiful."

The most important decision of Loyd's life was made. From this time on he would have a different relationship to God. And he

17

would have a different relationship to other people and to the world God had created. Things would never be the same again.

Loyd's baptism proved more eventful than anyone anticipated. There was no stream a person could be baptized in. And few country churches then had baptistries as do many churches today. Tall windmills that turned in the ever-present prairie winds pumped water from deep underground into large surface tanks. These tanks could serve as places for baptisms.

The water in the tank chosen for Loyd's baptism was deeper than the eight-year-old boy was tall. If he stood on the bottom, not even the top of his head poked above the surface. This situation presented a challenge to Loyd's father. But he hit upon what seemed to him to be a simple solution. He decided to let Loyd stand on an apple box.

The only difficulty was that the apple box wanted to float. So Pop Corder solved that problem by sliding his right foot into the end of the apple box which rested on the bottom of the tank. There! The box was steady, and Loyd could stand on the top, putting his head above water.

The members of the congregation and other friends circled the tank so each could have a good view. Only adults and tall children could see over the edge of the tank. Smaller children had to be held up by their parents.

As he always did, Brother Corder, Loyd's father, explained what baptism means. He explained why a Christian should be baptized. Then he prepared to lay Loyd backward until the water washed over his face.

When he did, his right foot came out of the box. The box popped to the surface of the water. Loyd went down much deeper than his father intended. The startled preacher struggled to set his spluttering son out of the tank onto dry ground.

All of that motion started a small tidal wave which swept to one side of the tank and then rebounded to the other. The spectators were caught flat-footed as the waves sloshed over the tank side and onto their Sunday finery.

Few of the people present that day ever forgot the day Brother Corder baptized his son. Loyd certainly never forgot the day. Even

18

though the hilarious way things went remained a vivid memory, he remembered something else even better. He remembered what his baptism meant. From that time on, he would try to please Jesus even though he had no idea how his life would turn out. He was just beginning to let God unfold the plan for his life.

He had no idea of the adventures which were in store for him. He didn't even know the names of the towns and cities which would be so important in God's plan for him. He did not dream of flying over much of the world. He had no idea of the great romance of his life. He only knew that he would love Jesus always.

The Garrison Year

Pop Corder finished his studies at Wayland Junior College. He knew that he still needed more education. He had no intention of giving up. But during the years in Plainview, he had gone in debt to stay in school and to provide for his family.

He decided to teach school for a year and pay off the debts. Garrison, New Mexico, had an opening for a teacher. There was just one opening because Garrison had a one-room school.

The Garrison schoolhouse was a white, wooden building which looked a lot like a church auditorium. A low stage was at the front of the room. The desks stood in rows facing the platform. The seat for each desk was hinged to the frame that supported the desk behind it. Each of the six grades had its own place to sit, and the teacher moved from grade to grade to hear recitations. Each of these recitations lasted fifteen to twenty minutes. Between recitations every pupil was expected to keep busy preparing for the next recitation.

Pop Corder had Loyd and about twenty-nine other pupils distributed through the six grades. Twenty-nine children watched to see how their teacher was going to discipline. Most of them figured that what he did with or to Loyd was their best clue to how they would be treated.

They got their first signals the day Loyd learned to whistle. Whistling did not come easy for Loyd. While Teacher Corder helped the boys and girls in other grades, Loyd practiced his whistling. He could practice while he read or did math problems.

One day to his own amazement Loyd emitted a shrill and prolonged whistle.

20

Immediately Teacher Corder was beside his desk. "Loyd Corder, was that you who whistled?"

Loyd replied, "Yes, Sir," without looking up.

"Stand up, Sir," the stern voice commanded.

Loyd stood up. He clenched his teeth and batted his eyes as his father reached for the paddle.

Whack! Whack! Whack!

"You may be seated now," Teacher Corder said.

"Yes, Sir," Loyd replied. What he wanted to say was, "Do I have to?"

The other children had watched what had happened to Loyd. It was enough to put them on their good behavior for a long, long time.

"Nobody ought to have his own father for a schoolteacher," Loyd told one of his buddies. "My father makes an example of me to keep the rest of you in line."

"Maybe so. Maybe not," his friend replied. "You are the one who whistled. And you do talk when he is helping the others."

"Yeah, I know," Loyd grinned. "And I am the one Teacher caught whittling on his desk."

Twice a year the pupils entertained the community. A curtain was rigged across the front of the stage so a play could be given. Between acts, other pupils recited poems and gave memorized speeches.

Loyd's entry into the world of stand-up comedy took place on that platform. "When I was born, we were twins," he recited. "We were so much alike that nobody could tell us apart. Unhappily one of us died, and nobody knows yet if it was me or my brother." The audience laughed. What Loyd learned about standing before an audience in that schoolroom would help him in standing before audiences at other times.

During the winter, Loyd had a second grand adventure with hog-killing. He knew what to expect as he helped butcher the two hogs his father had raised. Loyd and his father placed the meat in a big wooden box nailed to the north end of their house. Each layer of meat was coated with a sugar-cure substance. As the meat cured out in the winter cold, it developed a smoked flavor.

Early one morning the excited yapping of their dog woke the family. The dog was on top of the meat box, barking furiously. Scarcely a hundred feet away stood a coyote. It smelled the curing meat. But when it saw Pop in the doorway, it turned and ran away. Even good meat like that was not worth being shot at.

That winter the Corders heated and cooked with cow chips. Wood was scarce on the plains. Borrowing a relative's team and wagon, they drove slowly across the pasture. The family members spread out and walked behind the wagon. Each carried a big burlap sack for collecting the dried chips. As fast as one bag was filled, another bag was started. Finally the wagon was full of sacks. Weary of their task, Loyd followed the wagon home and helped Pop lace the sacks against one end of the house.

Through the winter, Loyd's job was to bring the chips into the house to burn for heat and for cooking. Sometimes that winter he had to remove drifted snow before he could open a bag. But having a warm kitchen was worth the work. That was especially so on Saturday nights when a large galvanized washtub was brought into the kitchen. Who could have stood a bath if the kitchen had been as cold as the open prairie!

The kitchen was always the warmest room. In fact, it was often the only warm room. All through the cold months, Loyd would dash into his room at bedtime. As quickly as he could, he would unsnap one suspender of his bib overalls, letting them fall to the floor. Just as quickly he kicked off his shoes. Like a flash he burrowed under the covers, wearing his shirt and long drawers. There was no heat at all in his room, but he would be warm until daylight.

During the year that Pop taught at Garrison, he was also the pastor of the church at Long. Eventually the winter passed and with it the school year. Through the summer, the family lived on a large farm in the Long community.

Then suddenly summer was over. Pop Corder was ready to return to his studies. This time the family headed for Simmons College at Abilene, Texas. None of them was more excited than Loyd—especially when he saw how they were going to move.

Abilene and Robert Lee

Pop Corder hired a truck for the move to Abilene. By the time the truck was loaded, it resembled Noah's ark.

All of the family's furniture and personal belongings were worked into place in the truck. Almost the last things to go in were some crates of chickens. The very last thing was a large crate that Pop himself built. This crate held the family cow. Friends and neighbors helped the Corders hoist the cow and her crate aboard the wagon.

They were off to Abilene—five Corders, a flock of chickens, and one bawling cow. The trip took two days. When night came, Pop pulled the truck to the side of the highway. Mrs. Corder stopped the family car behind the truck. There the curious caravan camped until morning and time to head east once more.

But first Pop fed the cow in her crate. Then he fed the chickens in their crates. Then he reached through the sideboards of the truck and between the slats in the cow's crate. He milked her right there. "That's how to have fresh milk for breakfast when you travel," Pop commented when he completed the task.

When Loyd went to school that fall, he was nine years old. He expected to be a third grader. The teachers in Abilene did not agree. They said that, although he did good work, he was terribly slow doing it. So he had to repeat the last half of the second grade.

Such problems became unimportant because so many exciting things began to happen. For one thing, Pop bought Loyd a young Angora billy goat for a pet. When Billy was big enough, Pop made a wagon and harness for him.

By the next summer, Loyd was using Billy to help him with some

24

of his chores. One day Loyd and Billy were busy hauling trash from the house to the dump. Before they completed their work, a sudden summer storm sent them scurrying for cover.

"There, Billy," Loyd said, patting the goat on its back. "I'll unhitch you and just tie you here to the tree until this shower's over."

In a few minutes Loyd brought Billy a pan of feed. But when Billy began to eat his food, all of the chickens decided to help him. Billy wasn't too happy with them, but there was little he could do.

Loyd walked over to Billy from the porch where he had been watching the shower. Giving Billy a pat on the head, Loyd commented, "That was a nice shower, Billy."

But Billy had had all the interference he wanted. "Bah-ah-ah," he bleated his answer. And just for emphasis, he reared on his hind feet. Then he lunged for Loyd's stomach.

"Ouf!" Loyd groaned as he fell to the ground. Over the frightened cackling of the flying chickens, Loyd could hear the excited giggles of Carrie and Dikki. All Loyd could do was to grab Billy's horns and hold on.

Loyd got his first pair of roller skates the next Christmas. Those roller skates became part of a money-making scheme. The family cow gave more than enough milk for the Corders. They began to sell some of the surplus milk. Loyd delivered milk to other parts of the city. As a rule, he skated with a quart bottle under each arm. Only once did he break a bottle while skating his milk route.

Before Jim Corder graduated from Simmons College, he became pastor of the Baptist church in Robert Lee, Texas. After his graduation, the family moved to this small ranch town sixty miles southwest of Abilene.

Here Loyd's school fortunes took an upturn. The teachers in Robert Lee thought ten-year-old Loyd was an exceptionally good student. Instead of placing him in the fourth grade, they moved him all the way to the fifth grade.

Loyd liked to roam over the hills around Robert Lee, hunting rabbits and other small game. One Sunday afternoon, he and his dog, Ring, cornered a skunk under a big rock. "Now what do I

26

do?" he thought to himself. Since it was Sunday, he was not permitted to use his gun. Still, it seemed a shame to let a skunk get away. So Loyd stood on top of the rock and poked at the skunk with a big stick.

Eventually Loyd managed to kill the skunk. But before the skunk breathed his last, he sprayed Loyd with "perfume."

Loyd and Ring headed for home. "Hi, everybody," Loyd yelled as he reached the house. The rest of the family had gathered on the porch where they had just opened a gallon of homemade ice cream. For a moment everyone froze. Then they began to scatter.

Loyd and Ring enjoyed the gallon of ice cream. But everyone else lost interest in any kind of food.

While Loyd lived in Robert Lee, he set up his own workshop. He was able to buy a few tools. Then he built a makeshift forge. He used the forge to heat nails, rods, and other metal objects to form the tools he could not buy.

One of his first projects was a steam engine made from discarded auto parts. It ran beautifully. The only problem was that it never developed enough power to do anything but run itself.

Loyd used the workshop for other projects. He made presents for others. He gave small, wooden chests to his aunt and each of his three sisters. Willie Fay, his third sister, had been born while they were in Abilene.

Loyd also made a perpetual-motion machine. Actually the machine never did move on its own, much less move forever. But it certainly produced some other motion—and emotion. Loyd left the machine in the hall where his mother stumbled over it!

Life in Robert Lee was not just fun and games. Loyd always had a number of chores to do. One of his jobs was to draw water from the cistern for all the household needs.

The Corder cistern was a large hole in the ground. Gutters on the house dumped water into the cistern whenever the rains came. Once the cistern filled, it never ran dry, not even in long dry spells.

But water doesn't run up hill, and there was no pump to carry it into the house. So Loyd drew water from the cistern a bucketful at a time, time after time, day after day.

During the years in Robert Lee, Brother Corder invited an old friend from Wayland College days to preach a revival meeting. As "Doc" Tennison preached, Loyd felt the Lord calling him to special service.

At the end of the service, Loyd went to talk with "Doc" Tennison. Then Loyd made an announcement.

"I'm surrendering my life to do whatever the Lord wants me to do." As he spoke to the congregation, he seemed bigger than he really was. His voice was firm, and he looked straight at the people, his blue eyes meeting their gaze without blinking.

Loyd knew he had made a promise to the Lord. He was not sure exactly what that commitment would mean.

"Lord, tell me exactly what it is you want me to do," became his prayer. But the Lord didn't give Loyd a direct answer. Several nights later Loyd slipped outdoors through the bright moonlight and into the shadows under a lacy mesquite tree. Again and again he asked the Lord to tell him exactly what he was to do.

Finally in desperation he prayed: "Well, Lord, it seems I just can't know what you want me to do. As you reveal it to me, I'm willing to try to do it." Suddenly his heart filled with the same deep peace he had experienced when he accepted Christ as Lord and Savior.

Loyd was sure God had a plan for his life of service. That plan would require him to use everything he had learned to the moment of his surrender to special service. And Loyd was yet going to learn much, much more.

Soon after this experience, Loyd went with his father to an associational meeting of Baptist churches near Ballinger, Texas. In the afternoon, a group put on a play. *The Heroine of Alva* was about Ann Hasseltine Judson. She and her husband were missionaries in Burma in the nineteenth century.

As he watched the play, Loyd began to feel that his call was to foreign missions. Loyd did not know of any other kind of missions. He assumed that his mission field would be China. That was the only mission field he knew much about.

Soon after the associational meeting, Loyd got an opportunity to follow the direction that had been set under the mesquite tree. His father called him in. "Son, the only way to learn to preach is to preach," he said. "So I'm going to arrange for you to preach your first sermon!"

Brother Corder set up time for Loyd to preach at a country schoolhouse across the Colorado River south of Robert Lee. When the Sunday came, Loyd dressed as carefully as he could. He took a piece of leftover biscuit from the cupboard. Stooping, he rubbed each of his patent leather shoes with the biscuit until he was satisfied with their shiny surface. Standing before the mirror, he worked long and hard to get his fine brown hair to lie flat.

Loyd and his parents reached the schoolhouse before anyone else arrived. For an awful moment, Loyd wondered what he would do if no one came. But eventually ten people were seated before him. After they sang for a while and prayed, the people sat silently waiting for the preacher to begin.

"Preacher boy, that is," one of the older men thought to himself as he watched the slender teenager. Loyd was never more than of average height for his age as a boy.

Loyd's text was John 3:14-15: "As Moses lifted up the serpent in the wilderness, even so must the Son of man be lifted up: That whosoever believeth in him should not perish, but have eternal life." Loyd explained the meaning of the passage in great detail. On and on he preached. Eventually he noticed his mother looking at her watch. Drawing his sermon to its close, he gave the invitation. No one responded.

On the way back to Robert Lee, he said, "Mother, I saw you look at your watch. How long did I preach?"

"Four minutes, Son," she said. "Four minutes."

Loyd still did not know clearly where God's plan would lead him. He had thought about missions. And he had preached his first sermon. These were only clues. God's plan would continue to unfold.

The Stockdale Years

In the summer of 1929, the Corder family prepared for another move. The First Baptist Church of Stockdale, a farming center in central Texas, called Jim Corder as its new pastor. That move took the family to an entirely different part of the state.

The Stockdale area was famous for fine Watson watermelons, cantaloupes, and tomatoes. So for a high school agriculture course Loyd rented five acres of land. He planted the acres in watermelon and cantaloupe.

When harvest came, Loyd borrowed a horse and wagon to move his melons to market. The wagon had narrow wheels which sank into the sandy soil as soon as Loyd put the first melon on the wagon. But Loyd didn't notice.

"Giddap," he yelled. The horse reluctantly moved his heavy load a few feet. Loyd hoisted more melons on the wagon as quickly as he could. Panting for breath, he leaned his slender body against the side of the wagon for just a moment. Straightening up, he pushed his hair back from his forehead before jumping onto the seat of the wagon.

"Giddap," he yelled again. This time the horse twisted his head to give Loyd a long look. His eyes seemed to say, "Can't you see this wagon is sinking every time you put on another melon?"

Several more times Loyd's loud "giddap" moved the horse to tug the wagon a few more paces. Finally the horse again looked at Loyd. "Something is going to break," the horse seemed to say.

Loyd didn't believe in letting a horse talk back to him. His usually mild blue eyes took on a glint. "Giddap," he yelled, slapping the horse across the back with the reins.

30

The horse eased his hind feet back a foot or two. Then he leaned forward with all his might.

Pop! The harness split. This time the old horse peered at Loyd, and Loyd got the message. It was, "I told you so."

For just a moment, Loyd stared back at the horse. Then a big grin and a loud laugh restored Loyd to his usual calm nature.

The melon project was a success. And Loyd learned not to overload a vehicle nor its source of power. This bit of good common sense came in handy when he later learned to fly an airplane.

Another chore Loyd had was milking. He became responsible for milking a very big, old cow. She was as wild and stubborn as Billy had been. She never would stand still to be milked.

"Pop," Loyd complained. "I can't handle that old cow. She's going to kill me one of these days."

"Think about it, Loyd," was Pop's calm reply. "I believe you can figure out a way to handle her."

Loyd took his father's advice. He determined to solve the problem. He rigged some boards to put around the cow's neck when she ate from the trough. This strange yoke kept her from backing away and running off. The boards also forced her to stand near the wall.

Once the stubborn cow was in place, Loyd slipped the milking stool in close to her. Then he butted his head into her flank, just in front of her hind leg. Shoving her against the wall with his head, Loyd managed to milk her. She could still shove him aside, but she could not kick him.

As a high school junior, Loyd had to choose an elective course. The choice lay between advanced math and Spanish. Mr. Long who taught the math course was tall, skinny, and not particularly handsome. Miss Gabriel, the Spanish teacher, was a beautiful brunette with lovely brown eyes.

Loyd chose the Spanish course. Before the semester was over, Loyd became truly interested in Spanish. This interest stuck with him all through his college years. Loyd did not then realize how important this interest was in God's plan for his life.

In addition to raising watermelons, milking the cow, and studying Spanish, Loyd found time for two other interests. They were debate and football. One year he and his debate partner won second place in their division in the district meet in San Antonio. As a football player, he had one distinction. When the coach stumbled during practice, Loyd grabbed one of his feet. The coach fell flat, making Loyd the only player who ever successfully tackled the coach.

One day Mom called to Loyd as he came in from school. "Loyd, come to the kitchen. I want to talk to you."

She looked at the young man who stood before her. Five feet, nine. Slender. Blue-eyed. Tousled brown hair. Plaid shirt. Plain wash pants.

"Loyd," Mom said, "you need a suit."

"A suit!" Loyd exclaimed, brushing his hair back. "Long pants? No more knickers?"

"Yes, Loyd, that's exactly what I mean. This time something very mature. You're getting to be a young man, you know."

Loyd stood to his full height. And he stood to his full height a few days later when he and Mom went to the men's department in a local store. Before they left, he was the proud owner of a double-breasted suit made of sturdy blue serge in a herringbone weave. He was beginning to leave boyhood and would soon be a full-grown man, truly a young man.

As he was growing into an adult, Loyd remembered his commitment to special service for the Lord. He continued to preach in country churches. His sermons grew longer. From time to time a boy or girl made a profession of faith at the close of a service. Loyd felt especially happy at such times.

He still thought about being a missionary. It seemed to him that the best places of service to Christ were surely in foreign lands. He continued to think about going to China someday.

Just where God was leading was not yet clear to Loyd. But he knew that the next step was college. He chose to go to Howard Payne College in Brownwood, Texas.

College, Romance, and Marriage

Loyd Corder, age eighteen, stood silently for a long time, looking up at the tower of the administration building. Its stones seemed to speak of dignity and permanence and learning. He felt small, young, and not nearly as smart as he did at his high school graduation. Then he turned and walked back toward his new home.

By the end of the first year of college, Loyd knew what his major would be. Spanish was his choice. He looked forward eagerly to at least one Spanish course each semester for the rest of his college days.

There was another subject Loyd loved as much as he did Spanish. That was Bible. At college he had new opportunities to study God's Word. Bible became his minor.

One morning Loyd woke up feeling weak. Later in the day he could scarcely climb the stairs to classes. The condition worsened. Loyd had developed a rheumatic heart condition. His condition became so bad that the doctor thought he would surely die. And Loyd thought so too.

He began to pray long and hard. At first he asked to be made well. Finally he was able to say to God, "Do whatever will bring glory to you." And that was when he began to recover.

Later he remarked to a friend, "I am convinced that no one is ready to live until he is ready to die." He had learned another important lesson.

Loyd's two interests, Spanish and Bible, came together in a special way. Loyd's father gave him the first Spanish Bible Loyd ever owned.

Actually all of Loyd's experiences were moving in the same direction. He got a new roommate. The new roomie's name was Pedro A. Hernandez [PAY-dro Ah ere-NAHN-dez]. Pete spoke Spanish, and he was the pastor of the Mexican Baptist Church in Brownwood.

Pete noticed several things about Loyd. One was that Loyd made friends with the children of his Mexican classmates. Second, Pete noticed that Loyd could read and write Spanish well. Third, Pete knew that Loyd was serious about following God's will for his life.

One day Pete said, "Corder, you know some Spanish. And I have more missions than I can take care of. I wish you would take care of the mission at Coleman."

Loyd saw no reason for not trying to help Pete. After all, he had preached in a Mexican church at Luling the summer before. And he had spoken at a Mexican Baptist associational meeting.

Loyd drove to Coleman, twenty-five miles away. He preached on the courthouse square on a Saturday. The large crowd that gathered to listen delighted him. But when the cotton-picking season was over, most of the people who made up the crowd moved away.

The Mexicans who lived in Coleman permanently were fascinated by the new gringo [GREEN-go] preacher. They asked one another, "What kind of a gringo is this? He can read and write Spanish, but he cannot talk or understand us when we talk Spanish."

Within a few weeks Loyd learned to talk with the people. Then the people said, "We have never seen a gringo learn Spanish so quickly." They gave Loyd the Spanish name Elogio Cortéz [ay-LOE-he-o cor-TEHZ].

At this time Loyd's sister Dikki (Leota) was a student at Howard Payne. She wrote Loyd that she was coming to Coleman, where he was living, with a group of students. They planned to give a program in one of the churches on October 5, 1939. Loyd made a point of attending the program.

As he entered the church, a young lady he had never seen before greeted him. "I guess you're Loyd Corder," she said.

She was Gertrude Levada Hiner, known to her friends as Trudy.

36

Loyd did not then suspect the important part Trudy was to play in his life. But he did know that he wanted to see her again—and again—and again.

Loyd began driving his Model A Ford to Brownwood as often as he could. At first he acted as if he were going to see Dikki.

On December 5, Loyd invited Dikki and Trudy to his church in Coleman. After the morning service, the three of them were guests in the home of a family named Martínez.

Mrs. Martínez did all she could to see that everyone enjoyed the meal. She knew that Loyd, like her own family, was accustomed to eating Mexican style. They all used folded tortillas to eat with instead of the usual knives, forks, and spoons. But she knew that the girls had never eaten this way. So she went to the main house on the ranch where she and her husband were caretakers. There she borrowed enough silver for them all.

During the afternoon Loyd made a date with Trudy to go on a picnic with some other young people at Lake Brownwood the following Tuesday. He didn't realize it, but he was definitely falling in love with the pretty girl from Fort Worth.

The next Tuesday just wouldn't come soon enough to suit Loyd. And when the picnickers were a bit slow in leaving Brownwood for the lake, he invited Trudy to walk with him along Buffalo Bayou, the only stream near the campus.

As they walked along, holding hands, Loyd blurted out, "Trudy, can you trill an *r*?"

"Silly," Trudy replied, "everyone can do that." Trudy had no idea what Loyd's question meant.

But Loyd felt God wanted him to work with Mexican people. He knew that he must not become too deeply involved with any girl who couldn't learn to speak Spanish. And no one ever speaks Spanish well without being able to make the special *rr* sound common in Spanish, but not used in English.

On the way back to the campus Loyd, Trudy, and another couple rode in the back seat of the car. Intrigued by this handsome, blue-eyed fellow, Trudy gave Loyd a little hug. Loyd was sure that she had more than just a passing interest in him.

About this time the Mexican Baptist Church at Big Spring

38

called Loyd to become its pastor. That meant that at Christmastime he had to make a long trip to see Trudy. But he was determined to see her. He was in Fort Worth with Trudy and her family on New Year's Eve.

To celebrate the New Year, Loyd and Trudy went to see a religious movie at a church. Before they left Trudy's house, they agreed to go by another church and bring Trudy's sister, Mary, home when the movie was over.

But after the movie, they drove to a hill overlooking a lake. Below them the lights of the city twinkled. And overhead the stars twinkled. Neither Loyd nor Trudy was aware of how rapidly time was slipping by. They talked about first one thing and then another.

Suddenly they heard the popping of firecrackers and the sound of factory whistles. Here and there a Roman candle or a skyrocket lit the dark spots across the city.

"Loyd, it's midnight. It's 1940," Trudy exclaimed.

Loyd decided to start the New Year right. Taking Trudy's hands between his, Loyd said very slowly, "If I bought you an engagement ring, would you wear it?"

For a moment Trudy was silent. Then she looked up at Loyd, saying softly, "I sure would."

When they arrived at the Hiner house, everyone was still up. "Let's tell your folks now," Loyd suggested.

But before they could tell their news, Mr. Hiner said, "Is Mary with you?"

For the first time, the excited pair remembered their promise. They looked at each other in dismay. "We, uh, uh," Loyd stammered. He wondered if poor Mary were still waiting in the church, all alone on New Year's Eve.

Then Mr. Hiner burst out laughing at the forgetful couple. "It's OK," he said. "My brother picked her up long ago. But," he added, "I would be interested in knowing just why you two forgot your errand." The twinkle in his eye indicated that he already had a pretty good idea of what he was about to hear.

Loyd returned to the Mexican church at Big Spring as an engaged man. During the rest of the winter, Loyd managed to go to Brownwood several times to see Trudy. They grew more and more certain that they were meant for each other. And they counted the days until summer when they planned to be married.

Only one other big event happened in Loyd's life that spring. He drove to El Paso to attend the Mexican Baptist Convention of Texas.

"Elogio Cortéz," the people happily greeted him.

During the convention, Elogio decided to cross the Rio Grande River to visit the Mexican city of Juárez. World War II had begun. The border was carefully watched to prevent spies from entering the United States. When Elogio returned to El Paso, someone at the convention wanted to know if he had trouble coming back across the river.

"No," Elogio responded in Spanish. "I had no trouble at all."

One of the women exclaimed, "Those border guards probably thought you were American."

Loyd knew that he had been accepted by his Mexican friends. He was no longer merely a gringo who could read, write, and speak Spanish well.

Trudy and Loyd set July 15, 1940, for their wedding date. The ceremony was held in Cowden Hall on the campus of Southwestern Baptist Theological Seminary. What a good setting for a couple who, in the church at Big Spring, would be working much as missionaries work!

Like most grooms, Loyd wanted to get away smoothly after the ceremony. He arranged with his cousin, R. D., to park his car on the east side of the campus. Loyd parked his own car right in front of Cowden Hall. He knew his and Trudy's friends would decorate it. Loyd grinned as he thought of how he and Trudy would dash to R. D.'s undecorated car and make a clean escape.

After the ceremony, R. D. slipped a key ring into Loyd's hand. When Loyd and Trudy reached R. D.'s car, Loyd saw that the key ring had about fifty keys on it! He frantically began to try first one key and then another in the car's locked door.

"Loyd," Trudy exclaimed, "we've got to do something quick."

The only escape they could see was a nearby house. They ran up the front steps and right into the living room. The lady of the house was in the room, playing the piano. She was surprised to see a bride and groom obviously just coming from or going to their wedding ceremony.

Breathlessly, Loyd and Trudy explained the situation. Their hostess assured them she would take care of things. With the key ring, she walked casually out to R. D.'s car. She tried the keys until she found the right one. Then she drove the car to the back of her house and turned it over to the new Mr. and Mrs. Loyd Corder.

College for both Loyd and Trudy was past. A new phase of life was beginning for the two of them. Their immediate future was awaiting them in Big Spring. Beyond Big Spring they could not know which way God would lead them.

A New Life Together

When the Corders arrived in Big Spring, only one of them spoke Spanish. But both of them were immediately involved in Spanish work. Trudy did not have to know Spanish to play the piano for the church.

Three months after the wedding, Loyd was called to be the pastor of the Mexican Baptist Church at Uvalde, Texas. Trudy and Loyd towed their belongings in a two-wheel trailer. They knew that they couldn't push their old car hard enough to make the 325-mile trip in one day. So they planned for one overnight stop. That's why they put their mattress and springs on top of the load in the trailer.

When dark came, Loyd pulled the car and trailer onto the wide shoulder of the road. With a bit of help from Trudy, he placed the springs and mattress on a level area. Loyd slept soundly, but Trudy stayed awake most of the night.

It seemed to Trudy that they had scarcely settled in Uvalde when Loyd was invited to consider a different kind of work. The job was director of city missions in Houston, Texas. Loyd agreed to go to Houston to talk with the missions committee there about the job.

Loyd wore his best suit, his wedding suit. And he wore his best shoes, his wedding shoes. When he saw that the committee had some well-known men on it, he remembered that both the suit and the shoes had been bought at a fire sale. The suit hadn't suffered particularly, but the shoes never would take a real shine. The longer Loyd talked with the committee, the more nervous he became.

All Loyd could say was: "I'm a country boy, and I don't know too much. I do know Spanish. I've never lived in a city. I don't know

42

what we will do except try to find out what the needs are and try to design some approach to it."

"That's just the kind of man we need," was the chairman's immediate response.

So once again the Corders moved. And Houston was a big change from West Texas. But Loyd and Trudy trusted God to lead them.

About a year later Dr. Jimmy Enete, a missionary to Brazil, came to Houston. Dr. Enete was a ventriloquist, and he used a dummy named Sammy in his work. Loyd was fascinated. "Why, I could do that," he thought at the time. Then he forgot about ventriloquism.

Like many missionaries the Corders sometimes had trouble managing on their rather small income. One day Trudy exclaimed to Loyd, "It seems like we have more money than we've ever had. Still I never do get to buy anything."

"Maybe you would feel better if you managed our money," Loyd suggested.

During the next month, Trudy bought some things she felt they needed. But at the end of the month, she was as upset as the month before. "I don't have enough money to pay my bills," she cried.

So Loyd and Trudy planned how to handle their money. They would watch the pennies, of course. And they would plan together for any big amounts of money they might spend.

In the fall of 1943, Dr. J. L. Moye, who was in charge of Spanish work in Texas, became ill. In 1944 Loyd was invited to help Dr. Moye with the work. A part of the agreement was that Loyd could attend classes at Southwestern Baptist Theological Seminary in Fort Worth.

Of course, this arrangement meant another move. Once more Trudy and Loyd packed their belongings in the same trailer that had followed their car all over Texas. As Loyd looked at it, hands on his hips, he couldn't help thinking of the way his father had packed their trailer for the move to Abilene so many years before.

44

Trudy stood silently with a small smile, thinking of the move to Big Spring and the move to Uvalde and the move to Houston.

"Well, Loyd," she said after a moment, placing a hand on his shoulder, "on to Fort Worth."

Both of them expected to spend several years in Fort Worth while Loyd completed his class work at the seminary. If they had realized what would soon happen, they might not have unpacked their things in Fort Worth.

The San Antonio Years

Dr. Moye's health became worse and worse and in a few months, he died. The Home Mission Board made Loyd superintendent of Spanish work in Texas, New Mexico, and Arizona. So the Corders moved to San Antonio, Texas—without camping on the way!

One day Loyd met a pastor who had also heard Dr. Enete and Sammy. This man had been as fascinated as Loyd. But he bought a dummy and learned the tricks of ventriloquism. Now he was ready for a better dummy.

"How about selling me your old dummy?" Loyd asked after he had carefully inspected it. With all of his skills, he knew he could keep the dummy in good working order.

What Loyd saw was a dummy about four and one-half feet tall with big brown eyes and stylishly long red hair. With his heavy eyebrows and bright red mouth, the dummy had a mischievous look that rather pleased Loyd. On his feet he wore brown shoes. In the back of his size 6X boy's suit was a hole so the ventriloquist could put his hand inside the dummy to do things like move his eyebrows and open his mouth.

Loyd waited while his friend tried to figure out just how much the dummy was worth to him. "I'll do it for $60.00," the man finally said.

"That's a deal," Loyd responded, "If you will let me pay you $15.00 a month until the dummy is paid for."

So Loyd bought the dummy who became famous as Joe Baptist. Loyd's pastor friend also threw in two books on ventriloquism. Loyd discovered that the two books did not agree. So he made up his own system.

46

From that time on, Loyd and Joe performed in many, many places. The places Joe enjoyed most were boys' camps. Joe liked to tell children how they could become missionaries and how Christians can help missionaries go all over the world.

Joe seemed real to children and adults when he "spoke." He winked if Loyd pulled the right cord inside him. One time a lady listened to Dr. Corder practicing a routine with Joe. Dr. Corder made Joe wink at her. The lady turned bright red.

Joe Baptist and Dr. Corder had several different routines. In one they talked about why there aren't more missionaries. They discussed what a person has to do to become a missionary and what kind of person he must be. Then they continued in this way.

DR. CORDER: Even if we had all the people we need to be missionaries, we don't have the money to send them out into the world.

JOE BAPTIST: Baptists have lots of money. They just won't turn loose of it. If they'd do what I do, there would be plenty of money.

DR. CORDER: Oh, do you give a lot of money?

JOE BAPTIST: No, but I do give a tithe. That is, I do when I have any money. But I don't often have any money.

DR. CORDER: I'm sorry about that.

JOE BAPTIST: No, you're not, or you would do something about it.

Of course, everyone laughed at this joke on Dr. Corder. When things settled down again, Joe Baptist asked Dr. Corder how he became a missionary. Then Dr. Corder told the audience many of the things you have read in this book!

Loyd and Trudy had no children. So in 1947 they adopted a baby boy whose parents were both Mexican. They named him Hiram Glenn.

At Christmastime, 1949, they adopted a second son. His father was Mexican and his mother was English. This handsome, dark-eyed baby they named Norman Edward.

Being parents helped Loyd and Trudy learn more and more about God's love. They realized better than before how much it cost God to give his only Son to save people from sin. They understood better than before that God can use each person's special talents

48

and skills in service to him. They learned better how to depend upon God to help them every day.

During the six and a half years in San Antonio, Loyd worked in the same way he told the Houston missions committee he would work there. He looked carefully at the needs of Spanish-speaking people throughout the Southwest.

He was soon aware of one need. Mexican pastors, Mexican church workers, and others told Loyd that Mexican church leaders needed education. Loyd joined others in saying, "We need special schools for our people."

Those who listened to Loyd and his friends agreed. In time, Loyd helped start two schools in Texas. One was the Valley Baptist Academy. It got its name from its location in Harlingen, a city in the famous Rio Grande Valley of Texas. The Rio Grande is the same river Loyd crossed as Elogio Cortéz years earlier to visit the Mexican city of Juárez.

The other school which Loyd helped to get started was called the Mexican Baptist Bible Institute. It was located in San Antonio. Today this school is a seminary attended by pastors and other church workers in Spanish-speaking churches from both the United States and Mexico.

Regular schools were not the only idea Loyd had for helping educate Mexican leaders. He began *La Escuela de los Profetas* [Lah ess-QUAY-lah deh los pro-FEH-tahs]. This title means "The School of the Prophets." Each year Spanish-speaking pastors and other church workers came together in San Antonio to study together for a week or two.

Education for Mexican church leaders was a great need. Still, both Loyd and Trudy could see another need. Many Mexican children living in the cities of the Southwest had no homes. Some were orphans. Some had been deserted by their parents. Some were runaways. To help these children, Loyd joined with others to start the Mexican Baptist Children's Home in San Antonio. Now the boys and girls at the home live in attractive houses on a lovely campus. At the home, Christian men and women help them grow up just as Christian mothers and fathers help their own children.

By the time six and a half years were gone, Loyd was thinking

49

about an old dream of his own. As he helped educate and train others, he thought of the kind of education he wanted for himself. And he began to plan.

In the fall of 1950, Loyd decided to return to school. Once more the family packed up the old trailer. "Wonder how many trips we'll finally make with this trailer," Trudy commented to Loyd.

"Not another one for several years," Loyd responded. He meant what he said. He expected to stay in Fort Worth, home of Southwestern Baptist Theological Seminary, until he earned a degree.

He was wrong again!

The Atlanta Years

A shrill ring startled Loyd from his studies. Putting aside his textbook and Bible, Loyd picked up the telephone. His mind was still more on what he had been learning than on what the call might be. He was doing his best to get a good start at the seminary.

"Hello," he said without too much enthusiasm.

"Loyd," came a familiar voice. "Courts Redford. We need someone to be secretary of the Language Missions Division. What would you think about joining us in Atlanta?"

Loyd squinted his eyes as he began to realize that he was talking to the head of the Southern Baptist Home Mission Board in Atlanta.

After the conversation, Loyd could hardly wait to talk with Trudy. This was such an unexpected invitation. It meant leaving seminary almost as soon as he arrived. Yet it might be just what God wanted him to do.

Loyd and Trudy talked about and prayed about this new challenge. Finally they decided that going to Atlanta was right for them.

"Seems as if the Lord has never let us stay in any one place long," Loyd commented.

"Well, we were in San Antonio for six and a half years," Trudy replied.

"And maybe we'll be in Atlanta about that long," Loyd added.

But he was wrong. Loyd worked for the Home Mission Board in Atlanta nearly five times as long as he worked any other place!

Soon after the Corders moved to Atlanta, Loyd decided to

improve Joe Baptist. "His head is too square," Loyd explained to Hiram. "I'm going to round it off."

Loyd picked up a wood rasp and began to run it back and forth across Joe Baptist's head. The wood began to turn to sawdust as Loyd filed away the sharp edges of Joe's head.

Hiram watched for a time. "Ouch, Daddy, ouch!" Hiram cried every time the rasp bit into Joe's head. To Hiram, Joe Baptist was more like a brother than a big doll.

Hiram's death a short time later was one of the hardest things that ever happened to the Corders. But they trusted God to help them, just as they always had.

During the second year the Corders lived in Atlanta, they adopted a baby girl. Mary Edith came to live with them in May 1952 when she was three and a half months old. Eddie became a big brother.

The work Loyd did for the Home Mission Board kept him on the go. When Eddie was small, he thought his daddy was gone almost all the time. And that fact troubled him. Mother didn't go off for days at a time. Why was Daddy gone so much? Finally Eddie looked at his mother's brown eyes. He looked at his own brown eyes in the mirror.

"Daddy," Eddie said when he was four. "I know why you have to travel. You have blue eyes."

Although Loyd seldom spent much time thinking of the important contribution he was making to language missions, others did. Loyd gave little thought to the great things he had done for Spanish-speaking people during his years in Texas. But others realized how important Loyd's work was and how well he had always done it.

Among those who recognized his work was the faculty of his old college in Brownwood, Texas. In 1952, Howard Payne College gave Loyd an honorary doctor's degree. Dr. Loyd Corder! Loyd could scarcely believe his new title. And no one knows exactly what Joe Baptist thought.

Being a home missionary did not limit Dr. Corder's influence just to the United States. Baptist work in Cuba and Panama were a part of the work of the Home Mission Board. Dr. Corder led mission work in these Spanish-speaking countries.

In 1955, he was invited to take Joe Baptist to Mexico. The two of them spoke at the Baptist seminary in Torreón.

That same year Loyd was invited to South America. He spent five weeks travelling in Venezuela. He spoke to many different groups and helped the missionaries with their problems.

In 1956, the heads of the Home Mission Board and the Foreign Mission Board made an important decision. Everyone believed that Southern Baptists should begin mission work in Puerto Rico. But no one was sure which Board should do the work on that island. Finally the Boards agreed for the Home Mission Board to start the work. Loyd became responsible for helping with work in another Spanish-speaking country!

One day in 1956, Loyd had to go from Atlanta to Philadelphia, Mississippi. He was to meet with the Indians who lived in that area. Philadelphia and Atlanta are not far apart as the crow flies.

But Loyd was not a crow. He flew by commercial airlines. He had to go to Pensacola, Florida, on the Gulf Coast and then to Jackson, Mississippi. There he had to get a car to drive the remaining miles to Philadelphia. By the time he reached the meeting, he was as tired as he could be.

"If I had a plane, I could have reached Philadelphia in short order," Loyd thought.

Actually Loyd didn't know how to fly a plane. Still the idea stayed with him. When he returned to Atlanta, he talked with Trudy about the possibility of learning to fly and of buying a small plane.

"But, Loyd," Trudy protested, "flying is dangerous." Then they talked about the advantages and disadvantages of Loyd's having a plane. They decided that flying a plane was safe and was far cheaper than commercial air travel.

In 1957, Loyd became the proud owner of an Ercoupe, and then he had to learn to fly. During the next twenty years he would own three planes. He flew the third plane, a Comanche, far enough to go around the equator thirty times. In that many hours of flying, he used up four engines!

Loyd bought his second plane after a long, long flight which

stretched from Atlanta to Prescott, Phoenix, and Tucson, Arizona. On the way back to Atlanta, Loyd decided to land at Philadelphia, Mississippi. For the first time in his flying career, he overshot the field. He waited too long before trying to climb back into the sky. When Loyd pulled back on the stick, the Ercoupe slid on the wet grass. The left wing hit a post. After bouncing around, the plane finally settled into a ditch.

Loyd walked away with only a bruise on his knee. But he had totaled the Ercoupe!

Trudy flew with Loyd at times—but reluctantly. One day she made a flight with him across the plains of central Texas. Between Waco and Fort Worth, Trudy was looking out the window, enjoying the view. Suddenly she realized that the plane's engine was spluttering. As she turned to Loyd with a question on her face, the engine stopped completely.

There was no sound now. Nothing but the soft whistle over the wings and body of the little plane.

"Look around, Trudy," Loyd said with too much calmness. "I've got to find a place to put this plane down."

Trudy knew this was no time to express the panic she felt.

"There's a field right over there," she exclaimed. With a hand that was about to shake, she pointed to a long, narrow cornfield. Doing her best to act as calm as Loyd was acting, she patted him on the back. "You're doing fine," she said deliberately.

Loyd glanced where Trudy had pointed and brought the plane around toward the field. It seemed to him and to Trudy that they were losing altitude too rapidly.

Fighting to avoid a crash, Loyd maneuvered the powerless plane toward an emergency landing strip. Trudy closed her eyes, braced herself, and prayed.

Down, down they drifted, feeling weightless. Trudy's eyes were still closed when the plane actually touched down.

As the plane bumped to a stop, she opened her eyes to see a muddy hayfield. They were not where she had expected to be. But they were alive. And the plane was undamaged. How thankful they were!

In good spirits, the Corders started to hike out of the field to a

nearby road. Then Trudy looked down at her feet. Her best, pink Sunday shoes were all muddy.

"Loyd Corder," she said angrily. "Look what you've done. You ruined my best shoes." Then both she and Loyd began to laugh.

Loyd took his flying as seriously as he did other things. He wanted to be the best. So he trained until he qualified for instrument flying. Then he equipped his plane with nearly all the instruments used on commercial airplanes.

Loyd Corder was always eager to save time in his travels. Not even traveling in his own plane saved enough time to suit him. So he bought a suitcase Honda. This small motorcycle can quickly be broken down into six parts. The six parts can then be packed in their own suitcase.

For four years Loyd packed the Honda into the plane, flew to his destination, unpacked the Honda, and cycled to his appointments. He would leave his office in Atlanta at 11:00 AM eastern standard time, eat a sandwich, ride the bike to the airport, pack it away, fly to Nashville. In Nashville, he would unload the bike and ride to the meetings. He would arrive in time for sessions at 1:00 PM central standard time. This means that the trip took only three hours in all. There was no delay for a taxi to or from the airport. He could even get back home from Nashville meetings in time for supper. In all, he rode that cycle 9,000 miles—another way he traveled for God.

In time, Loyd Corder's influence on missions went even beyond the foreign countries which spoke Spanish. In 1976 Roy Davidson, a missionary in Africa, invited Loyd Corder and Joe Baptist to Botswana. The nation was celebrating its tenth birthday, and the missionaries wanted Baptists to help with the celebration. While he was in Africa, Loyd also visited in South Africa, Zambia, Tanzania, and Kenya.

In 1979, Loyd received a request from an old friend. The widow of R. G. Van Royen asked him to help her carry out one of her husband's wishes. Mr. Van Royen wanted his portrait to hang at the Baptist seminary in Panama because he had started that school.

"Could you do this thing for me?" Mrs. Van Royen asked.

When Loyd agreed to help, Mrs. Van Royen gave him the oil

58

painting. He took it to Atlanta. For six weeks, Loyd wondered how he would get the painting to Panama.

Then he called the Foreign Mission Board and talked to Dr. Charles Bryan.

"I'm going to Panama soon," Dr. Bryan said. "If you'll bring the portrait to the Atlanta airport, I'll take it to Panama."

When Dr. Bryan reached Atlanta, Loyd Corder met him. The two men spent some time visiting and sharing ideas.

"You know, Charles," Loyd commented, "when I retire, I'd like to go to Spanish-speaking countries and help them."

"We could easily use you for a year in Mexico," Charles Bryan replied enthusiastically.

After Loyd Corder retired in 1981, he and Trudy went to Mexico. They were Mission Service Corps volunteers. This means that friends and churches helped to pay the expenses of the months they spent in Mexico.

Beyond Retirement

Loyd and Trudy Corder made the trip to Mexico in their eighteen-foot-long recreation vehicle, a Winnebago. With the rack for the Honda, the Winnebago is twenty-one feet long. And it is seven feet wide.

Many times Loyd had to be very careful driving the large vehicle through the narrow village streets. "The Winnebago needs a shrinker," he thought as he inched slowly up or down a street and around a sharp corner.

During the time in Mexico, the Corders lived in the Winnebago. Equipped with all the comforts of home, it gave them a good place to eat, study, sleep, and read. Trudy could practice her music on her electronic keyboard while Loyd pounded away on his type-writer.

Loyd introduced himself in the villages by a new Spanish name. It was more like his English name than the one he had been given long ago. The name he used was Bejamín Cordero [ben-ha-MEAN cor-DEH-row].

The Corders' ability to speak Spanish made them feel at home in Mexico. And this ability also made the people feel comfortable with them.

In the spring of 1982, the Corders returned to their home in Atlanta. Once things had settled down again, Trudy asked Loyd a big question. "Loyd," she said, "now that you've retired and we've completed this tour in Mexico, what comes next?"

"Well, you know I want to write an English version of the book I wrote in Spanish. I'll call it *The Beauty of Baptist Unity*."

Just then Trudy realized that the postman had just put some

61

letters in the mailbox. When she checked to see what was there, they discovered a letter.

"Trudy," Loyd exclaimed. "This is an invitation from the Baptist convention in Spain. They want us to come help them in 1983 for about six months."

Trudy laughed. "I'll check to see if we can take the Winnebago," she commented. "Or shall we just go on the Honda?" she teased.

Later at supper Trudy said, "I have another question for you, Loyd."

"Shoot," Loyd replied as he continued eating.

"Well, I've just been wondering what you will tell our grandchildren when they ask you about your life."

Loyd looked thoughtful for a moment. "If I complete another project I have in mind, I can give them a book to read about my life. I really want to write the story of my life."

Trudy smiled. "They'd enjoy reading about where you were born and your adventures, like killing the skunk . . . "

"And falling in love with you, Trudy, and getting married," Loyd said, reaching out to hold Trudy's hand.

"But," Trudy wanted to know, "what will you tell them about your life as a missionary, about our life?"

Again Loyd looked thoughtful. "I want them to know that I went into Mexican mission work perfectly happy. I never expected to do anything else. I am not certain what I am going to do in the future, but I can look back and see how well God has taken care of me.

"And I'd like them to know that the Lord called me to serve him, but he did not show me all at once what I would be doing all my life. He used many events and people to set the direction of my life."

Trudy patted Loyd's hand. With a smile she said, "With that and with the book about your life, I believe they'll want to listen for God's call for their lives too."

Remember

1. How did different people help Loyd decide to become a Christian?

2. How did he get started in Mexican mission work?

3. How many different talents and skills can you name that Loyd used in serving Jesus?

4. Which of the stories about Dr. Corder did you enjoy most?

Now think about these questions. They will be answered in your life as you continue to grow.

1. What is the most important thing you learned about missions and missionaries as you read the book?

2. How can you best serve God right now?

3. Do you think you might like to volunteer to be a missionary when you grow up? Will you be ready if God calls you, as he called Loyd Corder?

About the Author

Hi! Let me tell you a little bit about myself and why I enjoyed writing this book for you. I teach boys and girls your age in Sunday School. And I have written some of the study materials many boys and girls use in Sunday School. Several years ago I wrote a book about Jesus that thousands of children have read.

So one reason I enjoyed writing this book is because it is for you and your friends.

The second reason I enjoyed writing the book is that Loyd Corder has been one of my friends for a long time. Writing about him gave me opportunity to visit in his home. And that was a real treat.

The other reason I enjoyed writing the book is I am excited about missions and missionaries. One time I got to spend a month in the Philippines helping missionaries and the Filipino people. And I have also helped Spanish-speaking Christians in the United States. I wanted to help you know about missions and to think about what being a missionary means.